JUST KIDDING!

Kitchen Capers

By Paul Virr
Illustrated by Amanda Enright
and Kasia Dudziuk

Published in 2020 by Windmill Books,
an Imprint of Rosen Publishing
29 East 21st Street, New York, NY 10010

Cataloging-in-Publication Data

Names: Virr, Paul.
Title: Kitchen capers / Paul Virr.
Description: New York : Windmill Books, 2020. | Series: Just kidding! | Includes glossary and index.
Identifiers: ISBN 9781508197935 (pbk.) | ISBN 9781538391228 (library bound) | ISBN 9781508197942 (6 pack)
Subjects: LCSH: Food--Juvenile humor. | Wit and humor, Juvenile. | Riddles, Juvenile.
Classification: LCC PN6231.F66 V577 2019 | DDC 818'.602--dc23

Contents

Going Bananas!

What do you call a monkey with a banana in each ear?
Anything you like—it can't hear you!
Why do bananas never feel lonely?
They always hang around in bunches!

Fast-Food Fun!

Why do french fries always win the race?

Because they're fast food!

Did you hear the story about the giant burger?

It was pretty hard to swallow!

An Apple a Day?

Which apple is like a Christmas tree?

A pine-apple!

Why did the apple burst into tears?
Someone had hurt its peelings!

How do you
make an apple puff?
Chase it around
the orchard!

How do you make
an apple turnover?
Push it down a hill!

A Pizza the Fun!

Waiter, do you think my pizza will be long?

No, I think it will be round!

Why did the student become a pizza chef?

He needed to make some dough!

What do young dogs like on their pizza?
Pup-eroni!
What's the best thing to put into a pizza?
Your teeth!

Silly Space Food

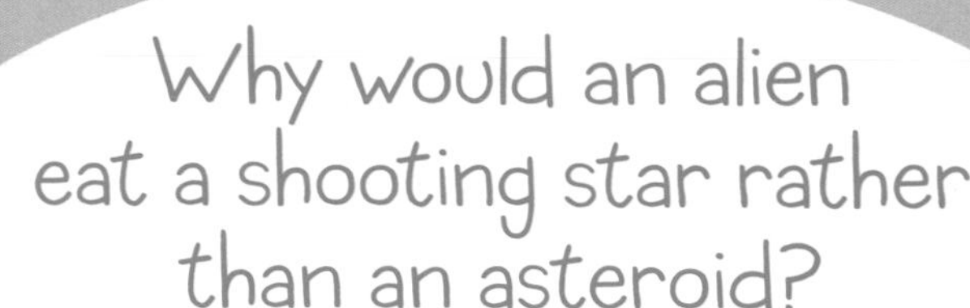

It's a little meteor!

What do astronauts put their food on?

Satellite dishes!

Dizzy Drinks!

Where can you get a milkshake?
From a nervous cow!
Why did the basketball player order cookies with his milk?
So he could dunk them!

Fruity Fun!

Why did the orange
stop in the middle of the road?
It had run out
of juice!

Which fruit do twins like to eat?
Pears!

What do you call a banana with an upset stomach?

A tooty fruity!

Soupy Loopy!

Waiter, why is the tablecloth all wet?

You ordered leek soup!

Waiter, what is this fly doing in my soup?

The backstroke, I think!

Waiter, this soup tastes funny.

So, why aren't you laughing?

Waiter, why is there a bee in my soup?

I'm sorry, it's the fly's night off!

Silly Sandwiches!

What do elves make their sandwiches from?
Shortbread!

Why couldn't the teddy bear finish its sandwiches?
It was totally stuffed!

What did
the golfer
eat at the picnic?
A club sandwich!

A Fridge Full of Fun!

Why did the tomato turn red?

It saw the salad dressing!

Why was the bean pod always running around?

He was full of beans!

What vegetable sounds like a parrot?
A carrot!
What did the salad say to get in the fridge?
Lettuce in!

Really Cheesy Jokes

What do witches spread on their bagels?
Scream cheese!
Which cheese do mice put on top of their pizza?
Mouse-zarella!

Glossary

apple turnover A dessert made from pastry filled with apple.

dough A mixture that is rolled out to make bread and pizzas.

fast food Food that can be prepared and served quickly.

meteor Small matter traveling in space at great speed.

satellite dishes Dishes that receive messages from satellites in space.

shooting star Another name for a meteor.

Index